the death

# of a honeybee

ella jayne

illustrations by megan boelter

Illustrations & cover art by Megan Boelter

ISBN: 978-1-7331593-0-2

First edition

to the ones who hurt me
and the ones who loved me
the ones who said i couldn't
and the ones who never doubted i could
thank you

table of contents

the death of a honeybee

i am content when
things are at peace. but when
there is danger
i strike in anger
and i am struck
by my own hand
dead.

full moon

when all feels lost
and out of control
and i wonder if my hands will
ever feel your skin again
the moon reaches down
and she whispers to me
that she will keep watch over you
until i kiss you again

star girl

constellations sparkle
in her eyes, and her
smile is radiant enough to
illuminate a whole
planet. sometimes i wonder if
i have to work at NASA
just to hold her hand.

but then she
blinks, her smile
falters, and i'm reminded that
she's only human, and that
every beautiful thing
that has ever been loved
lived and died
under the same sun.

falling

i never fell in love with you.
i had every intent
to love you;
and every dark corner of
my heart lit up
when you let me.
no, i didn't fall in love.
i closed my eyes, and
allowed you to gently
guide me into love
with you.
i didn't think that you
would guide me off of a
cliff.
i didn't think that you
would watch me fall
and laugh.
but you did.
and i have never recovered.

writer's block

i think what we call
writer's block isn't so much
trouble with writing,
but really it's
trouble with living

poison

i promised my mother that
i would stay away from
poison.
but she never told me
poison could speak my
name like it was sweet
hot chocolate or whisper
delicious words in my
ears until i lost my
grip on my heart.
from the moment i
met you i knew
there was no staying
away from you.
if only i knew then
the venom you held
in your tongue.

fall

there's a tree outside my window.
i live on the fourth floor, close enough
to reach my hand out the window and
touch its leaves.
the leaves at the top are starting to turn yellow.
"i can't wait for fall," i say,
and think i mean it.
but as i stare at these color-changing leaves,
i wonder if summer
is afraid of dying.

my cancer blood

i was born on a hot summer day.
middle of july,
middle of the night,
middle of two people with so much love between them
it overwhelmed me.
i was born beneath the starlit sky
beneath a constellation called
cancer.
fancy charts and online quizzes
will tell me i'm sensitive,
emotional,
quick to overreact but
slow to trust.
they're right about that.
my emotions are always in flux.
and maybe that's just the cancer in me,
but i think it's more
because of the depression.
my mood will tank in a second and
my palms will sweat like the Amazon
but my smile will shine just as bright as before.
i've always been good at faking it.

but, the truth is, the only time i feel happy
is when i'm sad.
strange, right?
i love being sad.
it just feels right.
it feels like the truth.
the only version of the truth that exists nowadays.
maybe that doesn't make sense.
let me explain.
cancer blood; overactive mind.
i've got trust issues.
overwhelming fear; fierce loyalty.
"describe yourself in four words"
is both my best friend and most fatal foe.
what do i do?
tell the honest truth?
deflect with a joke?
"i'm bad at math."
"living is too hard."
four words isn't enough,
and it's too much.
depression constantly haunts me.
whispers in my ear,

"you're not good enough."
"they don't love you."
"nobody would miss you."
"you deserve the pain."
my cancer blood beats through my veins
in four-word phrases
pumping malice into my fingertips
and whispering self-hatred into my skin.
i've always felt things strongly.
i suppose this isn't any different.
my cancer blood gives so much love
and will never take it in return.
my cancer blood won't allow me to be loved.
and sometimes, honestly,
i wish i'd been born a leo.

time machine

if i had a time machine
i would go back to the day
i was born
minus nine months
and give my father
a condom.

an attempt at art

i'm trying so fucking hard to
turn my pain into something
beautiful, like the sunrise
after a long, hard night.
i'm trying to put into
words the feelings that are
drowning me in noise.
i'm trying so hard,
i swear.
but it's so fucking hard.
how can i put into words
the density of the
storm clouds hovering over my head,
the immense tidal wave of
self-doubt crashing over me
day after agonizing day?
how can i explain to you
just what it feels like to
doubt your own memory, to
be so uncertain
that your own reflection
seems foreign?

how can i write about
something i'm not even sure
really happened the
way i remember it?
how can i villainize
someone i had the
misfortune of trusting?
how can i make you
believe a certain
version of the truth
when i can't even believe it myself?
believe me, i'm trying.
i swear to you, i'm trying.
but when my mind is
playing tricks on me
and i can't tell what's
real anymore
how can i sit down
and make it into something
beautiful?

writer's block part II

i think, perhaps i'm
trying too
hard to write something
amazing, when really i
should just write
something true.

it's my fault

all i know is that it was
naïve of me to
fall in love with you, when you were
nothing more than a
shape in the fog.

you know what you did

how can i ever
trust someone again with
my body,
when everyone's hands
become yours
when i close my eyes?

scream

you stole my voice
that day, broke the hand
that holds the pen
and i was silent.

but no more.

today, i speak
louder than ever
and i drown out all the
lies you ever told me.

equilibrium

today,
i've had as many laughter attacks
as panic attacks.
they balance each other out,
i suppose you could say.
somehow it doesn't feel that way.
it feels more like they come as one.
that tucked within the folds of the laughter
is a fear that will leave me paralyzed.
and every rush of giggles
is a precipice i walk with caution,
for one wrong step could send me
hurtling over the edge.

perspective

my heart broke the day
i learned that my
everest is some people's
rock bottom.

i hope it hurts

i'm trying not to be angry anymore.
you've seen my anger;
felt the sting of
words, angrily typed
on my phone keyboard, as
i tried to fathom how
you could have
done what you did.
i'm trying not to be angry anymore.
but it's so fucking hard.
i spent three years
being angry.
how can i know
anything else?
so i'm trying something new.
i'm trying to be honest.
and, if i'm being
honest,
i hope you never know
love
the way you could have
with me.

in all honesty, i hope
he breaks your fucking heart.
i honestly hope
i find you someday, shivering on
my doorstep,
begging for me back,
so i can slam the door in
your face, just like
you did.

fingerprints

you left your fingerprints
on my skin when you
left. you never wanted me to
forget about you.
but, my love,
i've burned them all away and,
with them, every
memory of you.

your last poem

when you left me, i
didn't write poems.
i just cried.
it seems that while i was
loving you, i forgot
how to write about
anything else.
it took a long time, but finally
the pen is back in my hand
and i'm writing
not about you
but about how wonderful life is
when you're not
in my world.

the first storm of spring

i don't know what i was after.
but when i heard the
sky shouting at me, i couldn't
ignore it. and so i put on a pair of
shorts, scars on full display, and
ran down the stairs to the backdoor.
i paused for a moment, wondering if
i was really crazy enough to go
outside during a storm so
violent it rattled the brick building
i call home.
then i opened the door.
it was cold.
drops of rain fell
heavy on my skin, kissed
my shoulders with
frigid lips as thunder roared and lightning
illuminated the sky and the
bare skeletons of the trees.
i let it consume me and
drench me from head to toe and,
amazingly, i felt free.

i don't know how long i was outside;
two minutes, maybe three. but
those precious few seconds
awakened something in me
i didn't know still existed.
so, as i stood there in the
storm, drenched and shivering,
i remembered that
i was alive.
and i was suddenly okay with that.

i used to live there

sometimes i go back
there and visit
my own burial site.
a place that once made me
swoon, now is
frigid with memory
and i see her, wiping
her face with
quivering fingers. when i
leave here, i am
alive. i wish
i could take her with me.

i've always wanted

to sit alone on a cold and
solid rock, to think of
nothing but the dreams
of the future, the things
not yet seen that are so
beautiful in thought.
to skim over the landscape
with unseeing eyes, gently reflect on
sounds that approach ears
red with the chill of the air,
a frost unnoticed by a mind
occupied by fantasies and possibilities.
to feel a smile widening rosy cheeks,
crinkling red eyes freshly
emptied of moisture.

to feel possible.
to feel probable.

i dream
simply to dream.
to wake up one day
not weighed down by fear, but
carried by the potential
for unfailing joy, feet moving
one after the other
into the future.
to feel my heartbeat as a
comfort rather than
a constant drum, every beat
moving me closer to my end.
to welcome tomorrow
with open arms.

to feel possible.
to feel probable.

wildflowers

they tell me i'll
find someone
but what i'd really like
is to find myself
in a field of wildflowers
with nowhere to be
but here

greyhound bus

i never realized how
beautiful snow could be
until i saw it out the window of a
moving bus.
i'm the kind of person who
complains during the first
snow, who trudges through
black sludge
muttering the whole way, who
refuses to shovel the driveway and
never buys warm enough gloves.
but inside this cocoon of
centralized heating, watching the
landscape zip by outside,
i see it in a
new light. i look at the way it
reflects the sun that lies
high in a cloudless blue sky
and it instills a certain
warmth within me i
never expected from something
that is, by definition,

cold as hell.
the trees are bare
but still standing and i
want nothing more than to
wrap my hand around a
branch and assure them that
spring will come again.
even when they have lost
everything to the frigid air,
spring will always come.

protagonist

i read books
upon books
upon books.
five at one time,
most times.
not because i'm too ambitious,
or because they aren't enough,
but because i'm waiting
for a character who makes me forget
that she's nothing more
than ink on a page.

writer's block part III

i think that

when you use

your heart

anything on the page

becomes art.

cashew

i'll never know you when
you were the size of
a cashew.
but i'll know you when
you're the size of
a newborn,
when you're handed to me and
all i know is love.
i'll know you when
you're the size of
your first A+
and we celebrate with
ice cream and a
late bedtime.
i'll know you when
you're the size of
heartbreak so vast you
don't know if you'll
survive it.
but you will.
i promise you will.
i'll know you when

you're the size of
a graduation cap,
an overstuffed van
driving hundreds of
miles to your new home,
leaving me behind and
i'll think of when i
could hold you in
my arms, and you couldn't
understand my words but
you could understand
my love.
and maybe that's more
important than when
you were the size of
a cashew.

my truth

never again will i read
another woman's poem and
wish to write like her
because how could i
write about a life that
isn't mine?

alive

suddenly, the sun
shines brighter than
it used to, and my
body is light, i'm writing
poems again, and i
breathe deeply
without pain

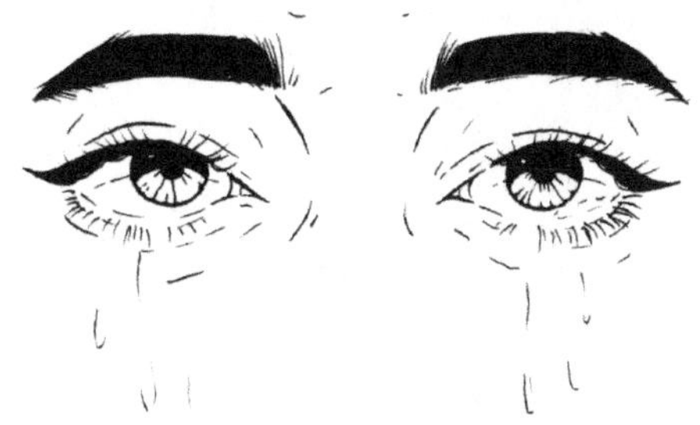

CPSIA information can be obtained
at www.ICGtesting.com
Printed in the USA
BVHW041428130122
626141BV00014B/1417